1998

First published by Appletree Press Ltd, 19-21 Alfred Street,Belfast BT2 8DL.

The Appletree
Yearbook

1998

ACKNOWLEDGEMENTS

The publisher wishes to thank the following for permission to reproduce work in copyright:

Sister Dwyer for *Between the Cliffs* and *A Quiet Read* by **Roderic O'Conor**; Kitty Casey for *Sunlight, 1925* by **William Orpen**; Tom Carr for *Children on the Front* by **Tom Carr,** Patricia Dalzell for *The Evacuation of Children* by **William Conor,** Gerard Dillon for *Self-Contained Flat* by **Gerard Dillon**; Jacqueline Donnelly and Lord Semple for *The Mother* and *The Red Hammock* by **Sir John Lavery**; *Women on Hillside* by **George Russell**; reprinted in part by the permission of Russell & Volkening as agents for the estate of George Russell. Rowel Friers for *The Poachers* by **Rowel Friers**; Lina Kernoff for *Boon Companions* by **Harry Kernoff**; Ciaran MacGonigal for *Early Morning, Connemara* and *Fishing Fleet at Port Oriel, Clogherhead* by **Maurice MacGonigal**; Sally McGuire for **Seamus Heaney** by **Edward McGuire**; Sadie McKee for *The Three Dancers* by **John Luke**; Barbara V Mitchell for *A Still Afternoon, Concarneau* and *Darning* by **William Leech**; Anthony O'Brien for *The White Dress* by **Dermod O'Brien**; Miss Richardson and Mrs Mills for *The End of the Glen* by **James Humbert Craig**; Dr Michael Solomons for *Rosapenna, Co Donegal* by **Estella Solomons**; James White for *The Wood* by **Jack P Hanlon**; Julius White for *Seán O'Casey* by **Augustus John**; Anne Yeats for *Flower Girl, Dublin* by **Jack B Yeats** and *Women and Washing, Sicily* by **Anne Yeats**.

While every effort has been made to contact copyright holders, the publisher would welcome information on any oversight which may have occurred.

For help in compiling this collection of work from the Ulster Museum, Belfast and the National Gallery of Ireland, Dublin, the publisher also thanks Alison Fitzgerald in the Nation Gallery of Ireland; Pat McLean, Rights and Reproduction Officer and Martyn Anglesea, Keeper of Fine Art at the Ulster Museum; and, Marie McFeely, Rights and Reproduction Officer, Adrian Le Harivel, Curator of British and Irish Paintings, Roy Hewson, photographer.

LIST OF ILLUSTRATIONS

LIST OF ILLUSTRATIONS

A Still Afternoon, Concarneau
William Leech

Rosapenna, Co Donegal
Estella Solomons

Seán O'Casey
Augustus John

Landscape with Cattle
Walter Osborne

*Detail of flowers from The Marriage of
Strongbow and Aoife*
Daniel Maclise

A Quiet Read
Roderic O'Conor

An Indian Lady, perhaps Jemdanee
Thomas Hickey

Children on the Front
Tom Carr

Curragh Chase House, Co Limerick
Jeremiah Mulcahy

The Regatta
Henry Robertson Craig

Sunlight
William Orpen

The Three Dancers
John Luke

A Vegetable Garden With Child in White
Walter Osborne

Two Children
Thomas Hickey

Flower Girl, Dublin
Jack B Yeats

Smithfield Market, Belfast
Cyril Clarke

Glenmalure, Co Wicklow, Sheep to Pasture
Nathaniel Hone the Younger

Kitchen Interior
John Mulvany

LIST OF ILLUSTRATIONS

MONDAY 29

TUESDAY 30 *D.C.!*

WEDNESDAY 31 *Early to 6pm at work, then an early night — and on New Year's Eve too!*

THURSDAY 1 *New Year's Day ~ late lunch with Eveline and Ronnie. Dinner with Angus and Jane.*

FRIDAY 2

SATURDAY 3 / SUNDAY 4 *Leak in kitchen, found on Saturday. Couldn't go home on Sunday as planned because of weather — snow/ice.*

Opening of Ringsend Docks

William Ashford (1746 - 1824)

The opening of the Grand Canal Docks at Ringsend in 1796 presented a grand and colourful spectacle and was recorded by the painter William Ashford that same year. As Lord Lieutenant, Earl Camden officiated. He is shown on the right conferring a knighthood beneath the Royal Standard. The Italianate canopied vessel in the foreground has been identified as the Earl's 'gondola', conveying a privileged few from sea to land. A leading exponent of the classical landscape tradition, Ashford's views were widely sought. This rather distinctive work in the artist's **oeuvre** *represents a valuable historical record and it was later acquired by the architect Francis Johnston.*

MONDAY 5 Mervyn - Continental Kitchens called re damage in kitchen. Floor has to be re-placed. Lifted vinyl, scrubbed floor and strained back!!

TUESDAY 6 D.C. cancelled. Quiet day. Collected Jane and then Eveline collected both of us. To Eveline's and had chinese and wine. Jim collected me.

WEDNESDAY 7 D.C. called. Possible trip to London — not confirmed. Delivery of oil. Jim called for a drink. Estimate from Mervyn £988.

THURSDAY 8 Estimate for vinyl from Martin Philips. 8-7 at work. Called with Mervyn to finalise details re kitchen. Ordered carpet tiles. Trip off. Insurance claim posted.

FRIDAY 9 Shopping.

SATURDAY 10 / SUNDAY 11

Detail of Wedding from The Marriage of Strongbow and Aoife, 1854

Daniel Maclise (1806 - 1870)

While his treatment of **The Marriage** clearly demonstrates Maclise's feelings about Ireland's subjugation in the twelfth century, his style is much influenced by the artistic trends of his day. The German Nazarene painters had stimulated a new interest in large scale subject pieces and he was also aware of French romanticism. The central couple are somewhat lost in the swirl of activity and portrayed with Victorian sentiment, as if unaware of the carnage around them. Recent painting **in situ** (because of its enormous size) has brought back the richness of the oil paint and allowed the fine detail to be seen again.

MONDAY 12

THURSDAY 15

TUESDAY 13

FRIDAY 16

WEDNESDAY 14

SATURDAY 17 / SUNDAY 18

Elegant Figures Drinking and Smoking in a Brothel

Herbert Pugh (fl 1758 - 1788)

This anecdotal image by the eighteenth century painter Herbert Pugh illustrates a lively brothel scene, where gentlemen indulge in debauched activity and are attended by two women. In the midst of the group a rather portly figure is slouched in a flushed stupor. He seems unable to withstand the pace of his more lively companions and is apparently oblivious to the smoke and noise surrounding him. A framed mythological subject on the right wall depicts a scene of related abandonment. Whilst Pugh exhibited landscapes in the main, he is credited with a number of satirical subjects, including **The Amorous Old Beau** *and* **The Procuress**. *Ironically his own intemperate habits hastened his death.*

MONDAY 19

THURSDAY 22

TUESDAY 20

FRIDAY 23

WEDNESDAY 21

SATURDAY 24 / SUNDAY 25

The Mother

Sir John Lavery (1856 - 1941)

This broadly-painted study of maternal tenderness was altered several times by Lavery over the years. It was begun in 1908 and completed the following year using a professional model for the figure of the mother. In 1924 he personalised it by repainting the main figure in the likeness of his daughter Eileen. The colour is very subdued, almost monochrome. The liberal use of black originates from Lavery's study of Spanish painting.

MONDAY 26

THURSDAY 29

TUESDAY 27

FRIDAY 30

WEDNESDAY 28

SATURDAY 31 / SUNDAY 1

The End of the Glen

James Humbert Craig (1878 - 1944)

Belfast born James Humbert Craig was largely self taught and drew his subject matter directly from the Irish landscape. He exhibited regularly at the Royal Hibernian Academy from 1916 until his death in 1944. His paintings reveal a particular affinity with the glens of Antrim and Donegal. An article in **The Studio** *in 1923 remarked on the burgeoning school of Northern landscape painters that their landscapes "though by no means emotional, are always most obviously sincere, closely observed, firmly and cleanly handled". The cloud formations which occupy over half of the pictorial space in this composition are rendered with a keen feeling for naturalism, revealing the artist's interest in painting out of doors.*

MONDAY 2	THURSDAY 5
TUESDAY 3	FRIDAY 6
WEDNESDAY 4	SATURDAY 7 / SUNDAY 8

The Wood

Jack Hanlon (1913 - 1968)

Father Jack Hanlon combined the careers of priest and artist. He had an interest in painting from his schooldays and later studied with the cubist painters Mainie Jellet and André Lhote. Their impact is clearly seen in his structured oil paintings, while his most expressive output was in watercolour, filling sketchbooks with a record of the people and landscapes seen on travels to the continent. The influence of the French Fauve painters is apparent in Hanlon's work after 1940. The flat patterns and dancing shapes in his rhythmic, colourful studies of still-life and landscape are among his most delightful images, evocative of the Mediterranean.

MONDAY 9	THURSDAY 12
TUESDAY 10	FRIDAY 13
WEDNESDAY 11	SATURDAY 14 / SUNDAY 15

Women and Washing, Sicily, 1965–66

Anne Yeats (born 1919)

After studying at the Royal Hibernian Academy between 1933-1936, Anne Yeats embarked upon a career in stage design, working for the Abbey Theatre and as a freelance practitioner. By the early 1940s, she had decided to become a painter and was closely involved with the Irish Exhibition of Living Art exhibitions. This work, painted after a visit to Sicily in 1965, conveys the intensity of the Mediterranean climate. Rows of washing, bleached by the intense sunlight, contrast with the dark, sombre tones of the women's garments. Though seated in relative proximity, they appear strangely distant, each one lost in contemplating private thoughts.

MONDAY 16	THURSDAY 19
TUESDAY 17	FRIDAY 20
WEDNESDAY 18	SATURDAY 21 / SUNDAY 22

Boon Companions

c 1934. Harry Kernoff (1900 - 1974)

The son of a Russian-Jewish furniture maker and a Spanish mother, Harry Kernoff was brought to Dublin when the family moved there in 1914. **Davy Byrne's** *was, and still is, a well-known literary pub off Grafton Street, Dublin. This shows the back snug, where favoured drinkers were invited as guests of the landlord, Davy Byrne, who appears in the centre. Kernoff himself stands on the left, while the other figure is Martin Murphy, a stage carpenter at the Gate Theatre, for which Kernoff designed sets. This Joycean subject is an unusual one for watercolour, but this version has an immediacy and freshness which the later oil version lacks.*

MONDAY 23

THURSDAY 26

TUESDAY 24

FRIDAY 27

WEDNESDAY 25

SATURDAY 28 / SUNDAY 1

The Provost's House, Trinity College, Dublin, 1820s

William Sadler II (1782 - 1839)

Active during the early nineteenth century, William Sadler is associated primarily with small view paintings like this view of the Provost's House, Trinity College in Dublin. Characteristically of Sadler, this painting was executed on a panel rather than a canvas support. The painting is topographical with the architectural features precisely rendered and the figures acting essentially as staffage to animate the foreground and middle distance. The Provost's House, designed by John Smith in the mid eighteenth century, is one of Dublin's finest Georgian townhouses and is decorated internally with noteworthy stuccowork.

MONDAY 2

THURSDAY 5

TUESDAY 3

FRIDAY 6

WEDNESDAY 4

SATURDAY 7 / SUNDAY 8

The Custom House, Dublin, 1817

Thomas Sautell Roberts (1760 - 1826)

James Gandon's Custom House quickly became one of the most depicted of Dublin's public buildings after its completion in 1791. Roberts offered a novel viewpoint in a broad panorama which includes St George's Dock and an array of ships. His original watercolour was engraved as an aquatint print and then handcoloured. As there were was no vantage point in this position, Roberts had to imagine it, exaggerating the perspective of buildings. He has already showed his aptitude for panoramic views in aquatints of Irish cities and rivers during the 1790s and two earlier Dublin views of the Four Courts and Trinity College.

MONDAY 9

THURSDAY 12

TUESDAY 10

FRIDAY 13

WEDNESDAY 11

SATURDAY 14 / SUNDAY 15

Interior with Members of a Family, 1750s

Philip Hussey (1713 - 1783)

An eighteenth century interior scene like this one, attributed to the painter Philip Hussey, affords the viewer an intriguing insight into contemporary taste. The elaborately patterned Turkey rug, distinctive keyhole fireplace and architecturally inspired wallpaper represent valuable records of material culture from eighteenth century Ireland. The framed paintings mounted on adjustable poles to either side of the fireplace were intended to act as screens, protecting women's faces from excessive heat. Although the identity of the family is not known, the portrait exemplifies a conversation piece, an informal type of group portrait popular during the eighteenth century.

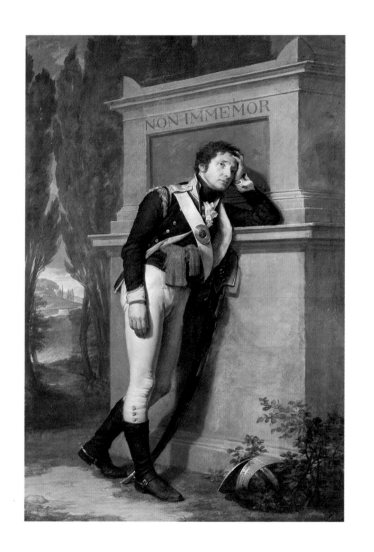

MONDAY **16**

THURSDAY **19**

TUESDAY **17**

FRIDAY **20**

WEDNESDAY **18**

SATURDAY **21** / SUNDAY **22**

Lt Richard St George Mansergh St George, c 1795

Hugh Douglas Hamilton (c 1739 - 1808)

Richard St George Mansergh St George (c 1756-1798) from Headford, county Galway, fought in the American wars before returning to Ireland. When his young wife Anne died in 1795, he determined to commission a portrait expressing "the expression of convulsive horror, Incurability, Delirium, I should say in my countenance". Hamilton, Ireland's leading neo-classical painter, avoids extravagant gesture to hint at the inner turmoil of the sitter, who rests by a funerary monument in a cypress grove, a discarded helmet at his feet. Mansergh St George survived only a few years after this portrait was completed and was hacked to death with a scythe during the 1798 Uprising.

MONDAY 23

THURSDAY 26

TUESDAY 24

FRIDAY 27

WEDNESDAY 25

SATURDAY 28 / SUNDAY 29

Claude Sketching, 1853

Daniel Maclise (1806 - 1870)

The work is a tribute to the French seventeenth century landscape painter Claude Lorrain. The youth depicted in Maclise's painting has been shown in a rather romantic light, sketching under the watchful gaze of an attractive companion, however an engraving after Joachim von Sandrart, Claude Lorrain's fellow artist, reveals that this is not a portait. Cork born artist Daniel Maclise established his career in London, rarely exhibiting in Dublin. In 1844, he was one of six artists chosen to decorate the Houses of Parliament in Westminister. He became a virtual recluse during his latter years.

MONDAY 30

THURSDAY 2

TUESDAY 31

FRIDAY 3

WEDNESDAY 1

SATURDAY 4 / SUNDAY 5

Self-Contained Flat

c 1953. Gerard Dillon (1916 - 1971)

From 1945 to 1968, Gerard Dillon lived mostly in London, where this was painted almost as a manifesto-picture. He found the freedom and the anonymity of London a relaxation from the narrow bigotry of his west Belfast youth, and the self-contained flat a symbol of this independence. He has shown himself three times, returning from work, cultivating the garden, and in the foreground, posing proudly with the tools of his trade as a housepainter - the pliers, screwdriver, blowlamp and a bottle of turps.

MONDAY 6	THURSDAY 9
TUESDAY 7	FRIDAY 10
WEDNESDAY 8	SATURDAY 11 / SUNDAY 12

Between the Cliffs, Aberystwyth

c1885. Roderic O'Conor (1860 - 1940)

*Born in Roscommon in 1860, Roderic O'Conor studied at the Dublin Metropolitan School of Art, the Royal Hibernian Academy, and later at the Antwerp Academy where he enrolled as a student in 1883. This coastal view near Aberystwyth is among the earliest surviving works by the artist. O'Conor has recorded the effects of sunlight on the headland with freely applied brushwork in broad fluid strokes, in a study redolent of **plein air** painting. He later settled in France where he remained longer than any other Irish painter of his generation. He developed a distinctive style of painting, characterised in the 1890s by an experimental use of colour and a striped or divisionist brushstroke technique.*

MONDAY 13

THURSDAY 16

TUESDAY 14

FRIDAY 17

WEDNESDAY 15

SATURDAY 18 / SUNDAY 19

Fishing Fleet at Port Oriel, Clogherhead Co Louth, c 1940

Maurice MacGonigal (1900 - 1979)

Port Oriel is a natural harbour on the Clogherhead headland, north of Drogheda. MacGonigal frequently painted along this part of the east coast from the mid 1930s when his mother's ill-health kept him in Dublin. The fishermen prepare their nets and sails for the night's work. MacGonigal has constructed an effective composition from the natural elements, applying his paint thickly and with a palette dominant with browns and reds. Fishing from Port Oriel was suspended during the war due to enemy activity, though MacGonigal continued to exhibit scenes of the harbour.

MONDAY 20

THURSDAY 23

TUESDAY 21

FRIDAY 24

WEDNESDAY 22

SATURDAY 25 / SUNDAY 26

Aileen Cox, 1916

Gerald Brockhurst (1890 - 1978)

*Gerald Leslie Brockhurst was born in Birmingham in 1890 and educated at the Birmingham School of Art and the Royal Academy.
In 1915, he moved to Ireland and a year later, this portrait was commissioned by Thomas Bodkin as an engagement present for his fiancée,
Aileen Cox. The sitter, lost in dreamy, wistful thought has been depicted against a mountainous backdrop although the work was in fact
executed in the Shelbourne Hotel, Dublin. Thomas Bodkin later became Director of the National Gallery of Ireland, a position which he
held between 1927-1935.*

MONDAY 27

THURSDAY 30

TUESDAY 28

FRIDAY 1

WEDNESDAY 29

SATURDAY 2 / SUNDAY 3

The Evacuation of Children, Great Northern Railway Station, Belfast

c 1941. William Conor (1881 - 1968)

A series of six or eight drawings illustrating Ulster's war effort was commissioned from Conor by the Ministry of Information in April 1940, for a fee of £50 plus £1 per day travelling expenses and a maintenance allowance for the time away from home. These drawings were exhibited in Brand's Arcade, Belfast, during **War Weapons Week** *on 2 December 1940. Another twenty-four drawings, including this, were bought directly from Conor by the Belfast Museum in 1941. Later efforts by Conor to obtain further commissions for Official War Artist's work met with a negative response.*

MONDAY 4

THURSDAY 7

TUESDAY 5

FRIDAY 8

WEDNESDAY 6

SATURDAY 9 / SUNDAY 10

A Still Afternoon, Concarneau

c 1910. William Leech (1881 - 1968)

The rich traditions, unique landscape and comparatively inexpensive cost of living, made Brittany a popular destination for Irish artists during the late nineteenth and early twentieth centuries. In the Breton town of Concarneau where this work was executed, both William Leech and John Lavery met their future wives. The cut off or cropped foreground elements in Leech's painting heightens the impression of immediacy, while a slightly elevated viewpoint affords a vista across the broadly painted water and beyond. Although Leech travelled widely on the continent he later acknowledged a debt to his early teacher Walter Osborne at the Royal Hibernian Academy, remarking simply that "he taught me all I needed to know about painting".

C.F.SOLOMONS 1931 .

MONDAY 11

THURSDAY 14

TUESDAY 12

FRIDAY 15

WEDNESDAY 13

SATURDAY 16 / SUNDAY 17

Rosapenna, Co Donegal, From Beachy Head, 1931

Estella Solomons (1882 - 1968)

Estella Solomons painted in county Donegal over many years. The village of Rosapenna on the Risguill peninsula, is viewed across Sheep Haven, in an area that is even more popular for visitors now. The sense of the wind and changing light is well suggested. Solomons' small, suggestive landscapes are in contrast to more academic portraits, which retain the impact of her training under William Orpen and Walter Osborne. She was a skilled etcher and had made a close study of Rembrandt after his Tercentenary exhibition. She exhibited landscape etchings and a similar linear quality also affected her oil paintings.

MONDAY 18

THURSDAY 21

TUESDAY 19

FRIDAY 22

WEDNESDAY 20

SATURDAY 23 / SUNDAY 24

Seán O'Casey, 1927

Augustus John (1878 - 1961)

*This intense portrait of the Dublin born playwright, Seán O'Casey, was painted by British artist, Augustus John as a wedding present. In the years immediately prior to the execution of this work, O'Casey's trilogy, **The Shadow of a Gunman, Juno and the Paycock** and **The Plough and the Stars** had been performed at the Abbey Theatre and provoked lively critical response. Famed for his imaginative use of the vernacular, O'Casey is shown in a rather serious attitude, his brow slightly furrowed. A large red handkerchief escaping from the playwright's pocket provides a vibrant accent enlivening the work.*

MONDAY 25	THURSDAY 28
TUESDAY 26	FRIDAY 29
WEDNESDAY 27	SATURDAY 30 / SUNDAY 31

Landscape with Cattle, 1892

Walter Osborne (1859 - 1903)

Landscapes generally appear in Osborne's work as the background of genre scenes and he may have been inspired to paint a scene of resting cattle by the work of Nathaniel Hone the Younger. The setting is probably north county Dublin and there is even a similarity of treatment to Hone. Osborne spent many years as a **plein air** painter in England and France but after 1893, he rarely left Dublin, where he had to support his niece Violet, whose parents had died. He found little patronage for landscape or what are now some of his most popular genre scenes of urban life.

MONDAY 1

THURSDAY 4

TUESDAY 2

FRIDAY 5

WEDNESDAY 3

SATURDAY 6 / SUNDAY 7

Detail of flowers from The Marriage of Strongbow and Aoife

Daniel Maclise (1806 - 1870)

*This detail represents a fragment of Daniel Maclise's monumental nineteenth century painting, **The Marriage of Strongbow and Aoife**. The subject is drawn from twelfth century Irish history and reveals the plight of the King of Leinster, Dermot MacMurrough, who sought help from the Normans in his battles against rival Irish lords. Strongbow succeeded to the throne of Leinster and was promised the king's daughter Aoife as a wife, in return for his help. This painting depicts the wedding which took place on the battlefield of Waterford in 1170. Maclise's meticulous, exacting approach is evident in this small foreground detail.*

MONDAY 8

THURSDAY 11

TUESDAY 9

FRIDAY 12

WEDNESDAY 10

SATURDAY 13 / SUNDAY 14

A Quiet Read, c 1910

Roderic O'Conor (1860 - 1940)

Roderic O'Conor had settled in Paris by the early 1900s, after a decade painting landscapes and peasant subjects with the Pont-Avon school in Brittany. He took up intimate interior scenes influenced by Pierre Bonnard. The woman reading is in dilute oil paint which creates the effect of an oil sketch, with the canvas showing through in places. It may seem unfinished but similar pictures were exhibited by him. A sense of repose and falling light is sensitively rendered in shades of pink and purple and the element of a mirror, adding an echo of the figure, is one he used often.

MONDAY 15

THURSDAY 18

TUESDAY 16

FRIDAY 19

WEDNESDAY 17

SATURDAY 20 / SUNDAY 21

An Indian Lady, perhaps Jemdanee, 1787

Thomas Hickey (1741 - 1824)

Thomas Hickey was a frequent prize winner at the Dublin Society Schools and had experience of study in Italy, but failed to secure adequate commissions for portraiture in Dublin. He moved to London where he contributed to exhibitions at the Royal Academy. In 1784, Hickey reached Calcutta where, over a period of seven years, he earned a distinguished reputation as a portrait painter among the British elite. The dignified Asian woman portrayed in this painting may be Jemdanee, the mistress of prominent Calcutta attorney, William Hickey (not a relation). The artist was later engaged as official portrait painter on Lord Macartney's expedition to Peking between 1792-1794.

MONDAY 22

THURSDAY 25

TUESDAY 23

FRIDAY 26

WEDNESDAY 24

SATURDAY 27 / SUNDAY 28

Children on the Front

c 1942. Tom Carr (born 1909)

After working in London with the realist Euston Road school of painters - William Coldstream, Claude Rogers, Victor Pasmore, Graham Bell, etc - Tom Carr returned to his native Ulster in 1939 and settled in Newcastle, county Down, where this was painted. This picture was bought by the Thomas Haverty Trust in 1942 and presented by them to the Belfast Museum, now the Ulster Museum. The soft handling and uncompromisingly objective observation are typical Euston Road practices.

MONDAY 29

THURSDAY 2

TUESDAY 30

FRIDAY 3

WEDNESDAY 1

SATURDAY 4 / SUNDAY 5

Curragh Chase House, Co Limerick, 1834

Jeremiah Mulcahy (c1804 - 1889)

Situated near Adare in county Limerick the landscaped environs of this century house were largely created by Sir Aubrey de Vere in the early nineteenth century. His son, also named Aubrey de Vere, was a noted Victorian author and poet whose archives, including manuscripts by Wordsworth and Tennyson, were destroyed when the house was gutted by fire in 1941. A native of county Limerick, Jeremiah Hodges Mulcahy secured a number of commissions from local landowners for views of their estates. The back-lit effect in his work with long shadows contrasted with sunlight, emphasises the verdancy of the idyllic landscape.

MONDAY **6**

THURSDAY **9**

TUESDAY **7**

FRIDAY **10**

WEDNESDAY **8**

SATURDAY **11** / SUNDAY **12**

The Regatta, 1958-59

Henry Robertson Craig (1916 - 1984)

Robertson Craig was born in Scotland and settled in Dublin after the war working alongside the artist, Patrick Hennessy. At a time when it was difficult to gain portrait commissions, Robertson Craig painted a conversation piece group of his close artistic friends and patrons which masquerades as a scene on a pleasure boat. Included are businessman and collector, Gordon Lambert (with his Rosall School blazer), gallery owner David Hendriks with his cousin Yvette, Major and Mrs Vernon, and the artist himself in profile beside fellow painter Patrick Hennessy. His carefully structured compositions have a richly worked surface and still suggest a photographic immediacy.

MONDAY **13**

THURSDAY **16**

TUESDAY **14**

FRIDAY **17**

WEDNESDAY **15**

SATURDAY **18** / SUNDAY **19**

Sunlight

c 1925. William Orpen (1878 - 1931)

*The relaxed, unselfconscious pose of the young woman in this painting lends the work a charming intimacy. Completed in William Orpen's studio during the mid 1920s, it includes a framed Impressionist work by Monet from Orpen's own collection. Shafts of sunlight playing on a background wall illuminate the room and animate the composition. Orpen advocated drawing from life, as well as sure drawing skills and craftsmanship. A successful portrait painter, he was also a gifted teacher, numbering artists Seán Keating and Margaret Clarke among his pupils. During the last decade of his life, he published two books **Stories of Old Ireland** and **An Onlooker in France**, the latter a memoir of the First World War.*

MONDAY 20

THURSDAY 23

TUESDAY 21

FRIDAY 24

WEDNESDAY 22

SATURDAY 25 / SUNDAY 26

The Three Dancers

c 1945. John Luke (1906 - 1975)

After studying in London, Luke returned to Belfast in 1931, where he became friendly with John Hewitt. Luke, who never married, lived with his parents in Lewis Street. He taught the life classes in the Belfast School of Art for many years (until 1973), and was renowned among the students for exceptional exactitude and strictness. He admired Eric Gill, and his drawings and sculpture certainly show this. In 1941 Luke and his mother were bombed out of Belfast and went to live at Knappagh, county Armagh.

MONDAY 27	THURSDAY 30
TUESDAY 28	FRIDAY 31
WEDNESDAY 29	SATURDAY 1 / SUNDAY 2

A Vegetable Garden with Child in White

c 1882. Walter Osborne (1859 - 1903)

A young child moving throughout the garden in this small oil painting by Walter Osborne seems almost lost in the vegetation, her slight proportions emphasised by the large, impressive cabbages before her. Like many of his nineteenth century contemporaries exposed to the naturalist tradition of painting on the continent, Walter Osborne favoured outdoor studies executed under natural light. Although drawn to landscape painting by inclination, the sensitivity and charm of his portraits ensured their popularity. Financial restrictions obliged him to accept portrait commissions. Osborne's career ended tragically in 1903 when, aged forty four, he died from pneumonia in Dublin.

MONDAY 3	THURSDAY 6
TUESDAY 4	FRIDAY 7
WEDNESDAY 5	SATURDAY 8 / SUNDAY 9

Two Children, 1769

Thomas Hickey (1741 - 1824)

The two unidentified children were painted following Hickey's return from a six year visit to Italy, when he was gaining a reputation in Dublin for portraits. At this young age, both girls and boys were dressed similarly; the apple held by one and the basket by the other may be to differentiate them. Hickey's figures are charming, if somewhat awkward. He was more skilled at small scale portraits at this date, with a richness of colour adopted from his knowledge of pastel. Later, he worked in London and Bath. His style changed radically after settling in India to paint the wealthy expatriates.

MONDAY 10	THURSDAY 13
TUESDAY 11	FRIDAY 14
WEDNESDAY 12	SATURDAY 15 / SUNDAY 16

Flower Girl, Dublin, 1926

Jack B Yeats (1871 - 1957)

Yeats treated the subject of flower girls on a number of occasions during his career. In this oil painting which dates to 1926, a pallid girl is shown in the centre of the composition offering a small collection of flowers to an elegantly dressed woman. Artificial light from a shop interior frames the figure of a gentleman, emerging on the left. The free expressive brushwork is characteristic of Yeats with textured areas or **impasto** *where the paint has been thickly applied. In her catalogue of the Yeats Collection in the National Gallery of Ireland, Hilary Pyle has noted that the artist adopted the rose as a personal symbol around this time, even securing one to his easel as he worked.*

MONDAY 17

THURSDAY 20

TUESDAY 18

FRIDAY 21

WEDNESDAY 19

SATURDAY 22 / SUNDAY 23

Smithfield Market, Belfast

Cyril Clarke (Irish, 20th Century)

This picture was given to the Belfast Museum in 1956. It shows the famous old covered market in the centre of Belfast, where curiosities of all sorts could be bought. The name dates from the eighteenth century and seems not to have been derived from the London meat market. The square was built about 1848, and given its glass roof by the Borough Surveyor in 1884. There were three arcades where the junk dealers had their stalls. The market was destroyed by bombing in 1974, and though it still exists, has lost its former charm. The area is now largely covered by the Castlecourt complex.

MONDAY 24

THURSDAY 27

TUESDAY 25

FRIDAY 28

WEDNESDAY 26

SATURDAY 29 / SUNDAY 30

Glenmalure, Co Wicklow; Sheep to Pasture

c 1880. Nathaniel Hone the Younger (1831 - 1917)

During the latter half of the nineteenth century, Paris and Antwerp became popular destinations for Irish artists seeking to continue their education. Nathaniel Hone the Younger's formative years were spent in France, first in Paris and later at Barbizon, on the outskirts of the forest of Fontainebleau. There, during the late 1850s and early 1860s he developed a **plein air** *approach to painting, based on direct observation of nature, and was influenced by French artists such as Corot. This mature work executed around 1880 after the artist returned to Ireland, is more sombre in tonality than many of his continental canvasses. A dramatic pool of light in the middle distance arrests the viewer's focus and highlights the figure of a lone shepherd marshalling his flock to safety.*

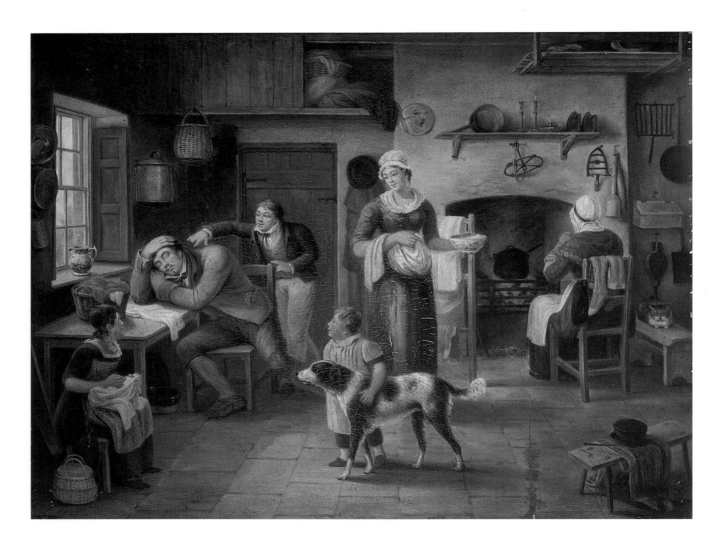

MONDAY 31	THURSDAY 3
TUESDAY 1	FRIDAY 4
WEDNESDAY 2	SATURDAY 5 / SUNDAY 6

Kitchen Interior, 1820's

John Mulvany (1766 - 1838)

At this date, there are few pictures of everyday Irish interiors. This kitchen scene is likely to derive from Dublin, where John Mulvany lived from 1810. He was a younger brother of the landscapist Thomas Mulvany and uncle of the Victorian portraitist, George Mulvany, but was less regarded as a painter. His slightly naive scenes offer instead a fascinating record of dress, kitchen implements and household linen, presented in a moral tone. Here the activity of the women is contrasted with the indolent husband who nurses a sore head from the previous evening's drinking.

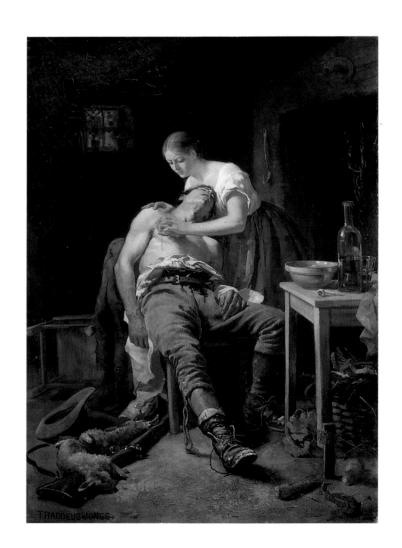

MONDAY 7

THURSDAY 10

TUESDAY 8

FRIDAY 11

WEDNESDAY 9

SATURDAY 12 / SUNDAY 13

The Wounded Poacher, 1881

Henry Jones Thaddeus (1859 - 1929)

Henry Jones Thaddeus was born in Cork. He studied at the Cork School of Art and Heatherly's Academy in London before travelling to Paris, as did many of his generation of Irish artists. This signed work was executed during his first year at the Académie Julian and was exhibited at the Paris Salon of 1881. Individual details like the strongly foreshortened pose of the injured youth and still life objects skillfully rendered, reveal the artist's competence at this early stage in his career in treating what would have been a daring subject back in Ireland.

MONDAY 14

THURSDAY 17

TUESDAY 15

FRIDAY 18

WEDNESDAY 16

SATURDAY 19 / SUNDAY 20

Women on Hillside

George Russell (AE) (1867 - 1935)

This barren hilltop in perhaps Donegal or Connemara presents a somewhat classically idealised pair of Irish peasant women. It came from the McNaughten family of Runkerry House, Bushmills, who possessed a number of Russell's pictures, some of which are now in the Ulster Museum. It contains stylistic elements which are reminiscent of certain nineteenth century English painters such as the Pre-Raphaelites and Miles Birket Foster.

MONDAY 21

THURSDAY 24

TUESDAY 22

FRIDAY 25

WEDNESDAY 23

SATURDAY 26 / SUNDAY 27

Connemara Cottages

Paul Henry (1876 - 1958)

An economy of means characterises Paul Henry's still landscapes of the west of Ireland. At the age of twenty two, Henry had the opportunity to study art in Paris, where he was stimulated by the work of Vincent Van Gogh and Jean François Millet. Following his return to Ireland, Henry brought new approaches to bear on Irish landscape painting and in 1920, he was a founding member of the Society of Dublin Painters. His rural landscapes like this view of **Connemara Cottages** *became synonymous with an idyllic profile of Ireland. In 1925, two of his paintings,* **Connemara** *and* **A View of Lough Erne***, were reproduced as travel posters for the London Midland and Scottish Railway Company. Despite the repetitive nature of Henry's later works, he was an influential figure and is regarded as one of Ireland's finest landscape painters.*

MONDAY 28

THURSDAY 1

TUESDAY 29

FRIDAY 2

WEDNESDAY 30

SATURDAY 3 / SUNDAY 4

The First Lock, Stranmillis

James Glen Wilson (1827 - 1863)

This example of the work of the little-known painter James Glen Wilson was bought in by the Museum in 1993, and its date of 1850 makes it his earliest dated picture. It shows the first lock on the Lagan Canal known as Molly Ward's, the traces of which can still be seen in Lockview Road, Stranmillis, near the boat clubs. The manager's two storey house is also still standing. At the time this place would have been bustling with cargo being transported between Belfast and the brickfields and collieries of county Tyrone.

MONDAY 5	THURSDAY 8
TUESDAY 6	FRIDAY 9
WEDNESDAY 7	SATURDAY 10 / SUNDAY 11

Rye Water Near Leixlip, Co Kildare

c 1855. William Davis (1812 - 1873)

The dexterity with which Davis has depicted the play of light on water distinguishes this nineteenth century oil painting. His treatment of reflections is both naturalistic and convincing, with the glassy river surface admirably conveyed. The location depicted represents a small tributary of the river Liffey some miles west of Dublin. Working with essentially earth tones of ochre, green and brown, Davis has created a work imbued with freshness and truth to nature. Although Dublin born, he spent the greater part of his career working in England where he exhibited with the Royal Academy between 1851-1872.

E McG. 1974.

MONDAY 12

THURSDAY 15

TUESDAY 13

FRIDAY 16

WEDNESDAY 14

SATURDAY 17 / SUNDAY 18

Seamus Heaney, 1974

Edward McGuire (1932 - 1986)

The poetry of Seamus Heaney (born 1939) is deeply earthed in his native Ulster. The award of the Nobel Laureate in 1996 was recognition of his broad vision, with reference to both the modern world and classical past. McGuire made this study prior to the full length portrait in the Ulster Museum. He grew up in a home full of modern art and after training at the Slade School, devoted himself to portrait painting in a stylised technique making a slow, painstaking analysis of his sitters. He depicted a number of literary figures, including poet Paul Durcan, and founder of the Dolmen press, Liam Miller

MONDAY 19

THURSDAY 22

TUESDAY 20

FRIDAY 23

WEDNESDAY 21

SATURDAY 24 / SUNDAY 25

Máire Nic Shiubhlaigh, 1904

John Butler Yeats (1839 - 1922)

This three quarter length portrait by John Butler Yeats was the first of two executed in 1904. Máire Nic Shiubhlaigh, an actress and patriot, performed at the Abbey Theatre and was noted for her accomplished portrayal of tragic roles. A perceptible softness in the modelling of the sitter's features, coupled with her dreamy, distant gaze, emphasises her celebrated beauty.

MONDAY 26

THURSDAY 29

TUESDAY 27

FRIDAY 30

WEDNESDAY 28

SATURDAY 31 / SUNDAY 1

Landscape with Fishermen, 1760s

George Mullins (fl c1756 - 1775)

Mullins trained at the Dublin Society Schools and initially painted snuff boxes in Waterford, before marrying the proprietress of the Horseshoe and Magpie alehouse in Dublin's Temple Bar. In 1763, he received a prize from the Dublin Society Schools for a landscape in oil and later for a history subject, marking the period of his finest work. His ideal compositions have carefully studied natural detail and lighting, and contain elements of rivers, castles and incidental figures derived from the Italian tradition. Such work was known in Dublin from original paintings and engravings, appealing to the eighteenth century connoisseurs. Mullins had a strong influence on his pupil, the landscapist, Thomas Roberts.

MONDAY 2

THURSDAY 5

TUESDAY 3

FRIDAY 6

WEDNESDAY 4

SATURDAY 7 / SUNDAY 8

Landscape with a Tree, 1943

Evie Hone (1894 - 1956)

Evie Hone's **Landscape with a Tree** reveals an obvious delight in strong patterning and vivid colour. In this late work painted in 1943, plateaus of land have been boldly defined in brightly coloured pigments, freely applied. Forms have been simplified and framed by darkened boundaries, like the flat geometric mountain projecting in the background. At the age of thirty three, following her training as a painter, Evie Hone began to work in stained glass and produced fifty windows and one hundred and fifty domestic panels during the last twenty years of her career. Along with Mainie Jellet, with whom she studied in Paris, Hone exercised a decisive influence on early twentieth century art in Ireland.

MONDAY 9	THURSDAY 12
TUESDAY 10	FRIDAY 13
WEDNESDAY 11	SATURDAY 14 / SUNDAY 15

The Red Hammock

Sir John Lavery (1856 - 1941)

This picture was altered by Lavery twice over a period of nearly thirty years. It was originally painted in 1907. In 1923 Lavery changed the face to that of his beautiful American wife Hazel. The paint surface later deteriorated, and the whole composition was completely repainted, with some more alterations, in 1936. It is a large, highly decorative picture, expressive of sun, luxury and the hedonistic French tradition which Lavery so much absorbed.

MONDAY 16

THURSDAY 19

TUESDAY 17

FRIDAY 20

WEDNESDAY 18

SATURDAY 21 / SUNDAY 22

James Joyce, 1919

Francis Budgen (1882 - 1971)

*The strikingly informal portrait of James Joyce was executed in 1919 and predates the publication of **Ulysses** in 1922. An inscription in the lower right corner reveals that it was painted in Zürich by Francis Spencer Budgen and the responses of both artist and sitter to the portrait were recorded in personal correspondence. Of his own work Budgen remarked that "the portrait does gives a true impression of the Joyce of the 'Ulysses' period - sprawling and seemingly relaxed but still alert and watchful". Joyce's observations were positive, with a humorously pointed corollary, "I like the pose in your portrait but for the love of Manfield tell the buyer that my size in shoes is a small seven".*

MONDAY 23

THURSDAY 26

TUESDAY 24

FRIDAY 27

WEDNESDAY 25

SATURDAY 28 / SUNDAY 29

The Poachers

c 1946. Rowel Friers (born 1920)

For many years Friers drew cartoons for the **Belfast Telegraph**, *and has also contributed cartoons to the* **Irish Times, Dublin Opinion, London Opinion and Punch**. *He has illustrated over thirty books, and has designed stage sets for the Lyric Theatre and the Belfast Grand Opera House. This was given to the Museum by the Thomas Haverty Trust in 1950. Friers showed paintings, illustrations and caricatures at the CEMA Gallery in Belfast in 1953, and in that year was elected Academician of the Royal Ulster Academy, at which he is still a regular exhibitor. He was elected its President in 1993.*

MONDAY 30

THURSDAY 3

TUESDAY 1

FRIDAY 4

WEDNESDAY 2

SATURDAY 5 / SUNDAY 6

The Stag Hunt, 1836

Francis Danby (1793 - 1861)

A contemporary of James Arthur O'Connor and George Petrie at the Dublin Society Schools, Franics Danby developed an early interest in landscape painting. In 1813, he moved to England where he later became an Associate member of the Royal Academy. An artist whose life was fraught with difficulties and domestic crises, Danby was compelled to leave England in 1829 and spent ten years on the continent, living in both Switzerland and France. In 1832, he reached Geneva with his mistress and their nine children. Painted in 1836, this fine, romantic work incorporates a view of the lake. The cool, pale tones of the still water establishes a dramatic contrast with the deeply shadowed foreground where details like the hunters, hounds and stag seem secondary to the majestic landscape.

MONDAY 7

THURSDAY 10

TUESDAY 8

FRIDAY 11

WEDNESDAY 9

SATURDAY 12 / SUNDAY 13

Darning, c 1933

William Leech (1881 - 1968)

Leech had a long career, strongly influenced by post Impressionism while he worked in France and where he stayed until the 1920s. Then, he forged his own style with individual figures or still-life frequently chosen as subjects. By 1933, he was working in London and often painted his companion May Botterell in his Hampstead studio, or in her nearby flat at 20 Abbey Road. She sits by the window or engages in domestic activities such as sewing and darning. The quiet intimacy and high viewpoint recall the figure studies of Edgar Degas, with Leech's own interest in the fall of light and evocation of the particular place.

MONDAY 14

THURSDAY 17

TUESDAY 15

FRIDAY 18

WEDNESDAY 16

SATURDAY 19 / SUNDAY 20

General William Cosby

c 1720. Charles Jervas (1675 - 1739)

William Cosby, sixth son of Alexander Cosby and Elisabeth L'Estrange was born at Stradbally Hall in county Laois. He became a Brigadier in the army and was Colonel of the Royal Irish Regiment. In 1731, he was appointed Governor of New York and the Jerseys. He noted that it caused him "more trouble to govern these people than I could have imagined". This distinguished portrait by Charles Jervas reveals the sitter's military associations, with a gleaming breastplate visible beneath his velvet coat. Jervas was originally from county Offaly. He established a successful career in England as a portraitist, visiting Ireland frequently. After the death of his teacher Godfrey Kneller in 1723, he became Principal Painter to the King.

MONDAY 21

THURSDAY 24

TUESDAY 22

FRIDAY 25

WEDNESDAY 23

SATURDAY 26 / SUNDAY 27

The Gate of the Cordelier Convent, Dinan, 1883

Joseph Malachy Kavanagh (1856 - 1918)

The gate is one of the few traces of the medieval Franciscan convent in Dinan, which is now a school. Both Walter Osborne and Kavanagh painted the same view of the cobbled entrance in the summer of 1883 and exhibited their representations the following year at the Royal Hibernian Academy in Dublin. After completing their training at the Antwerp Academy, they went to Brittany in search of picturesque subjects. Kavanagh's skill in depicting the fall of light across the outbuildings is evident, but he was less assured with figures, often painting them from behind and repeating this soldier in another picture.

MONDAY 28	THURSDAY 31
TUESDAY 29	FRIDAY 1
WEDNESDAY 30	SATURDAY 2 / SUNDAY 3

Figures and Animals by Classical Ruins, 1732

William Van der Hagen (fl 1722 - 1745)

*This painting of figures and animals framed by classical ruins was executed by Dutch artist William Van der Hagen, who came to Ireland in the eighteenth century. Van der Hagen's subject is in the manner of a **capriccio**, or imagined view, and conveys a pastoral idyll. In the foreground of the painting, a smiling barefoot peasant sways to the music played by her male companion. In the middle distance, contented animals rest and are tended to near the water's edge. The golden light suffusing the scene coupled with the classical landscape setting receding into the misty distance, contribute to the atmosphere of rarefied harmony which pervades the work.*

MONDAY 4

THURSDAY 7

TUESDAY 5

FRIDAY 8

WEDNESDAY 6

SATURDAY 9 / SUNDAY 10

Castletownshend, Co Cork, 1903

Egerton Coghill (1851 - 1921)

Sir Egerton Coghill came from Castletownshend, county Cork, and exhibited many landscapes derived from the surrounding countryside. Like many Irish artists, he studied at the Académie Julian in Paris and also worked at Barbizon. He exhibited in Dublin from 1882-1919 but did not need to earn his living as an artist and did not look for public recognition. He was particularly attracted by the romantic glow suggested in the seasonal colouring of spring and autumn in county Cork. He married the sister of Edith Somerville, who was a near neighbour with co-writer Martin Ross at Drishane House.

MONDAY 11

THURSDAY 14

TUESDAY 12

FRIDAY 15

WEDNESDAY 13

SATURDAY 16 / SUNDAY 17

Early Morning, Connemara

c 1965. Maurice MacGonigal (1900 - 1979)

The landscape and portrait painter Maurice MacGonigal began his artistic career in the stained glass studios of his uncle, Joshua Clarke. In 1923, he was awarded a three year scholarship to the Dublin Metropolitan School of Art where he studied under Patrick Tuohy, Seán Keating and James Sleator. From the early 1930s, MacGonigal's views of Connemara were exhibited at the Royal Hibernian Academy where he later served as President between 1962-1977. This view of Mannin Bay, painted towards the end of his career, reveals the comparative freedom of his later years. To the left of the composition, a lone figure stands watching over a scattered flock of sheep. Typically of MacGonigal, the rugged west of Ireland landscape has been rendered with integrity.

MONDAY 18

THURSDAY 21

TUESDAY 19

FRIDAY 22

WEDNESDAY 20

SATURDAY 23 / SUNDAY 24

The White Dress (Lady Farrer), 1920's

Dermod O'Brien (1865 - 1945)

O'Brien, the son of a county Limerick landowner, was one of the last Irish artists to train at the Antwerp Academy. O'Brien became an establishment painter in Dublin and successor to Walter Osborne and William Orpen as a society portrait painter. The study for the untraced full length of Lady Farrer is in a tonal style reflecting the work of James Whistler. The touch of Japanese style in the sunshade, and play on reflection in the mirror, are typical of the period, as is the formal dress, at a time when convention determined changes for each part of the day.

1997

January
M		6	13	20	27
T		7	14	21	28
W	1	8	15	22	29
T	2	9	16	23	30
F	3	10	17	24	31
S	4	11	18	25	
S	5	12	19	26	

February
M		3	10	17	24
T		4	11	18	25
W		5	12	19	26
T		6	13	20	27
F		7	14	21	28
S	1	8	15	22	
S	2	9	16	23	

March
M		3	10	17	24 31
T		4	11	18	25
W		5	12	19	26
T		6	13	20	27
F		7	14	21	28
S	1	8	15	22	29
S	2	9	16	23	30

April
M		7	14	21	28
T	1	8	15	22	29
W	2	9	16	23	30
T	3	10	17	24	
F	4	11	18	25	
S	5	12	19	26	
S	6	13	20	27	

May
M		5	12	19	26
T		6	13	20	27
W		7	14	21	28
T	1	8	15	22	29
F	2	9	16	23	30
S	3	10	17	24	31
S	4	11	18	25	

June
M	2	9	16	23	30
T	3	10	17	24	
W	4	11	18	25	
T	5	12	19	26	
F	6	13	20	27	
S	7	14	21	28	
S	1	8	15	22	29

July
M		7	14	21	28
T	1	8	15	22	29
W	2	9	16	23	30
T	3	10	17	24	31
F	4	11	18	25	
S	5	12	19	26	
S	6	13	20	27	

August
M		4	11	18	25
T		5	12	19	26
W		6	13	20	27
T		7	14	21	28
F	1	8	15	22	29
S	2	9	16	23	30
S	3	10	17	24	31

September
M	1	8	15	22	29
T	2	9	16	23	30
W	3	10	17	24	
T	4	11	18	25	
F	5	12	19	26	
S	6	13	20	27	
S	7	14	21	28	

October
M		6	13	20	27
T		7	14	21	28
W	1	8	15	22	29
T	2	9	16	23	30
F	3	10	17	24	31
S	4	11	18	25	
S	5	12	19	26	

November
M		3	10	17	24
T		4	11	18	25
W		5	12	19	26
T		6	13	20	27
F		7	14	21	28
S	1	8	15	22	29
S	2	9	16	23	30

December
M	1	8	15	22	29
T	2	9	16	23	30
W	3	10	17	24	31
T	4	11	18	25	
F	5	12	19	26	
S	6	13	20	27	
S	7	14	21	28	

1999

January
M		4	11	18	25
T		5	12	19	26
W		6	13	20	27
T		7	14	21	28
F	1	8	15	22	29
S	2	9	16	23	30
S	3	10	17	24	31

February
M	1	8	15	22	
T	2	9	16	23	
W	3	10	17	24	
T	4	11	18	25	
F	5	12	19	26	
S	6	13	20	27	
S	7	14	21	28	

March
M	1	8	15	22	29
T	2	9	16	23	30
W	3	10	17	24	31
T	4	11	18	25	
F	5	12	19	26	
S	6	13	20	27	
S	7	14	21	28	

April
M		5	12	19	26
T		6	13	20	27
W		7	14	21	28
T	1	8	15	22	29
F	2	9	16	23	30
S	3	10	17	24	
S	4	11	18	25	

May
M		3	10	17	24 31
T		4	11	18	25
W		5	12	19	26
T		6	13	20	27
F		7	14	21	28
S	1	8	15	22	29
S	2	9	16	23	30

June
M		7	14	21	28
T	1	8	15	22	29
W	2	9	16	23	30
T	3	10	17	24	
F	4	11	18	25	
S	5	12	19	26	
S	6	13	20	27	

July
M		5	12	19	26
T		6	13	20	27
W		7	14	21	28
T	1	8	15	22	29
F	2	9	16	23	30
S	3	10	17	24	31
S	4	11	18	25	

August
M	2	9	16	23	30
T	3	10	17	24	31
W	4	11	18	25	
T	5	12	19	26	
F	6	13	20	27	
S	7	14	21	28	
S	1	8	15	22	29

September
M		6	13	20	27
T		7	14	21	28
W	1	8	15	22	29
T	2	9	16	23	30
F	3	10	17	24	
S	4	11	18	25	
S	5	12	19	26	

October
M		4	11	18	25
T		5	12	19	26
W		6	13	20	27
T		7	14	21	28
F	1	8	15	22	29
S	2	9	16	23	30
S	3	10	17	24	31

November
M	1	8	15	22	29
T	2	9	16	23	30
W	3	10	17	24	
T	4	11	18	25	
F	5	12	19	26	
S	6	13	20	27	
S	7	14	21	28	

December
M		6	13	20	27
T		7	14	21	28
W	1	8	15	22	29
T	2	9	16	23	30
F	3	10	17	24	31
S	4	11	18	25	
S	5	12	19	26